Safety in Numbers

By the same author

Poetry
Summer with Monika
As Far As I Know
That Awkward Age
The Way Things Are
Everyday Eclipses
Collected Poems
Selected Poems
It Never Rains
joinedupwriting

Penguin Modern Classics
The Mersey Sound *(with Adrian Henri and Brian Patten)*

For Children
80
Poetry Pie
Sky in the Pie
Until I Met Dudley
Dotty Inventions
Bad, Bad Cats
Good Enough to Eat
The Bee's Knees
All the Best *(selected poems)*
Slapstick
An Imaginary Menagerie
Lucky
Mind the Gap
Money-go-Round
Crocodile Tears

Theatre
Tartuffe
The Hypochondriac
The Misanthrope

Autobiography
Said and Done

Safety in Numbers

ROGER McGOUGH

VIKING
an imprint of
PENGUIN BOOKS

VIKING

UK | USA | Canada | Ireland | Australia
India | New Zealand | South Africa

Viking is part of the Penguin Random House group of companies
whose addresses can be found at global.penguinrandomhouse.com

First published 2021
001

Set in 11/13pt Dante MT Std
Typeset by Jouve (UK), Milton Keynes
Printed and bound in Great Britain by Clays Ltd, Elcograf S.p.A.

The authorized representative in the EEA is Penguin Random House Ireland,
Morrison Chambers, 32 Nassau Street, Dublin D02 YH68

A CIP catalogue record for this book is available from the British Library

ISBN: 978–0–241–51735–2

www.greenpenguin.co.uk

Penguin Random House is committed to a sustainable future for our business, our readers and our planet. This book is made from Forest Stewardship Council® certified paper.

This book I dedicate to

. . . .

Safety in numbers?
Not any more.
The room starts to fill?
I'm out of the door.

Contents

Some Questions Regarding the New Bicycle

What was it like for you
when twenty-nineteen
parked its bicycle in the hall?

Did you take advantage?
Go for a spin in the spring?
Cut a swathe through leaves in the fall?

Or did it get in the way?
Add to the clutter of your life?
Take up valuable room?

A gift-horse to bump into
as you stumble from month to month
in the thickening gloom?

And what will you remember of 2019?
A Royal letting the side down?
Brexit? Trump? Democracy in reverse?

Floods in Yorkshire? Riots in Hong Kong?
Bush fires in Australia?
Cheer up. It can't get any worse.

Or can it?
A planet feeling its age and under strain
as veering, and out of control,
2020 comes careering down the lane.

This Summer, We Will Not be Taking a Holiday Abroad

How good not to be waiting for the cab
that will take us to the airport. Will the cat
still be here when we get back?
Is the house secure? How good

not to be in line waiting to go through Security.
Why must I take my belt off? Are my shoes offensive?
Do I look like a terrorist? Of course, I understand,
but really . . . How good

to avoid the frenzy of boarding. The boredom
of the inexplicable delay. The pain of feigning
nonchalance, the practised pretence
of being engrossed in a novel.

How I will miss the certainty of a bumpy flight,
the possibility of death by fireball.
How good not to be thankful for a safe arrival
and the cab waiting to take us somewhere.

Somewhere safe and sanitised where
we will throw away our masks and socially
distance ourselves from survivors
we half recognise from previous years.

The same cab that will take us back to the airport
and a plane to another airport, and a cab
to the house and the cat who hadn't noticed
our absence. How good.

Seaside Staycation

We made it to the beach at 5 a.m. and set about our tasks.
Mine to erect the windbreaker using anti-bacterial masks
The kids to build sandcastles in a circle round our plot
While my wife dug out the trench then went to fetch the Rot.

(We call it Ruby, though the dog is a he,
as fearsome as a borrowed Rottweiler can be.)

Safe in our bubble, no super-spreaders we,
Anti-social distancing we had down to a T.
Lying low on our lilos, the kids on their phones
Ruby barking at seagulls or gnawing at their bones.

At 8 a.m., music blaring, we were settled and prepared
To scare away the vanguard of the incoming herd.
The Union Jack fluttering marked our domain
When, at 8.15 precisely came the first drops of rain.

What began as a breeze turned into a gale
The spatter of raindrops, the staccato of hail.
A hurricane in a hurry came within reach
As clouds retched and threw up all over the beach.

The trench filled with water, the sandcastles subsided
When the windbreaker took flight, we took fright and decided
Enough was enough, so we lowered the flag,
Wrapped it round our pasties and stuck it in the bag.

The car park, a marina with a single white boat
Our van as it happens, already afloat.
Seaside staycations? Never again.
The day after tomorrow we're leaving for Spain.

How to Live Longer

In Parliament today, the Minister for Mists
and Mellow Fruitfulness announces
that as a result of the pandemic
there will be no autumn this year.
September, October and November
are to be cancelled, and the Government
to bring in the nine-month year instead.
Thus, will we all live longer.

Emergency measures are to be introduced
to combat outbreaks of well-being
and feelings of elation inspired by the season.
Breathtaking sunsets will be restricted
to alternate Fridays, and gentle dusks prohibited.
Fallen leaves will be outlawed, and those found
in possession of conkers imprisoned without trial.
Thus, will we all work harder.

The announcement caused little reaction.
People either way don't really care,
no time have they to stand and stare.
Either looking for work, or slaving away,
just another lockdown day.

Adultery in Isolation

This is not the time for adultery.
Your lover will fail to be impressed,
not so much by the face mask
and stale musk of sanitising gel,
but your flouting of the rules.

Have you not listened to the radio?
Read the news? Has the Minister
for Health been talking to himself?
Does the two-metre rule not apply
to serial adulterers? Get a grip.

Go home and self-isolate. Resort
to self-abuse for all our sakes.
And when the time comes and it's over
(not soon enough I imagine
for pickpockets, pole-dancers,

bouncers, drug dealers and the like.
Not to mention health-care workers,
nurses, doctors, kids, mums and dads),
then, and only then can you pick up
the phone. Good luck.

Father Knows Best

In my cellar I have enough food
for at least six months. Medicines,
wi-fi, video games and a chemical toilet.
No room on this island for Shakespeare
or the bible. Under lock and key
the tools necessary for a life after death.
I have carried out my instructions to the letter.

Most evenings I'm down here. Checking
the stores, masks, breathing apparatus.
Cleaning and polishing. My wife, bless her,
thinks I'm obsessive, like other men
about cars or football. But deep down
she understands. I have no hobbies.
My sole interest is survival.

Every few weeks we have what I call DD,
or Disaster Drill. At the sound of the alarm
we each go about our separate duties:
Disconnecting services, switching off the mains,
filling the casks with fresh water, etc.
Mine is to oversee everything before finally
shooting the dog. (This I mime in private.)

At first, the kids enjoyed the days and nights
spent below, it was an adventure. But soon
they became bored and began to question
the project. Mutterings about community,
care for the elderly, the poor and the like.
But I am firm. Father knows best,
and soon enough they'll grow to thank me.

Beneath my bunk I keep an Armalite rifle
loaded and ready to use one fine day
when panicking neighbours and so-called friends
try to clamber aboard. The ones who scoff,
who ignore the signs. I have my orders,
there will be no stowaways. No gatecrashers
at my party. A party starting soon.

And the sooner the better. Like a grounded
astronaut I grow daily more impatient.
Am on tenterhooks. On my knees each night
I pray for closure. Ask Gaia to get on with it.
I fear sometimes she has forsaken us.
We her favourite children, meek, drilled
and ready to inherit an Earth newly cleansed.

I scan the headlines, watch the screen.
The latest outbreak, violence on the streets,
mass burials. Saddened, of course, but thrilled
at the prospect of a new eco-world order.
From the children's bedroom, a cough.
Persistent and unsettling. My wife rushes in.
I rise and go to the cellar. Double-lock the door.

After you. No, after you

The winding path, soon face to face,
eyes fixed, you quicken your pace.

Who backs off, who goes through?
Bad luck! You feel the smugness,

it sticks like glue. Practising your scowl,
you continue on. That was then

and this is now. Social distan
cing brin ging uscloser.

The winding path, soon face to face,
you stand down, wave them through.

What's the hurry? '*No, after you.*'
A smile shared. Sticks like glue.

There's a Hole in My Trainer

The trouble started when I noticed a hole
in the right toe of my black Nike trainers.
I managed the problem by ensuring that
I always wore a pair of black socks.

All went well until I noticed a hole
in the toe of one of my black socks.
I managed the problem by wearing
the offending sock on my left foot.

Perhaps it should come as no surprise
but I was unprepared for the shock
of discovering one morning
an unsightly hole in the other sock.

The remedy? Black nail varnish
on the peeping big toe. It worked a treat.
Enabling me to work out and jog
without drawing attention to my feet.

Sadly, when the nail bar on the high street
closed I was thrown into a dilemma.
A spot of darning? Gaffer tape on the toe?
I did as I always do: Think outside the box.

Went online. Bought a new pair of socks.

Audio Nature Trail

I responded to an invitation to help champion the environment by recording an audio nature trail for a reserve on the Green Belt at the border of London and Surrey known as Farthing Downs and Happy Valley, an area famous for its wildflower meadows and ancient woodland. On Wednesday, 15 July 2020, I recorded the script in my study, using an iPhone.

Record
'Hello, and welcome to the Happy Valley and Farthing Downs Nature Trail.'

Pause
The recording gets off to a promising start, the voice, warm and inclusive, before the first of the aeroplanes elbows its way through the clouds, adjusts its face mask and lunges towards Heathrow.

Record
'The hedge to your right is composed of aspen trees, their leaves trembling in the slightest breeze. In 1866 it is said that a Lincolnshire lass, seeking to be cured from a fever, pinned a lock of her hair to an aspen tree, saying . . .'

Pause
One of the Polish builders on the roof next door stops shouting to switch on a generator. Followed by an electric drill. It grinds to a halt.

Record
'"Aspen tree, aspen tree, I prithee to shake and shiver instead of me."'

Pause
Almost faultless except for my calling it an Aspirin tree. **Delete**.
I am about to press **Record**, when the radio on the roof is
switched on and a track by Abba drowns out the intermittent
birdsong. Fingers in ears, I put my head out of the window and
mouth a ribald Liverpudlianism.

Record
*'It was also believed that if a cutting from a fingernail was pressed
into the bark of an aspen by someone suffering from a disease,
they would be cured by the time the bark grew over the nail.
Further along, the hedge is mainly formed from blackthorn, a thick,
impenetrable hedge favoured by birds for nesting.'*

Pause
I am on a roll. Unfortunately, so is the 16.05 to Waterloo.
The window rattles in its wake. Pause to put kettle on.

Record
*'In this field you might often catch sight of the red kite, with that
characteristic deep red/orange colouring, or those other impressive
birds of prey, buzzards, which nest in the woodland nearby.
Listen out for their distinctive mewing call.'*

Pause
That is, if you can hear it above the sky-shudder of another plane.
As if called to prayer, the electric drill joins in.
Make tea and play back recording. Panic.

Record
*'Well, time is running out for us now, so might I just clear up
a few concerns you may have. You thought you heard
snatches of "Dancing Queen"? If so, no doubt being sung
by a pack of Scouts and Guides on a camping adventure,
Abba still being very popular among woodcraft folk. A train?*

No. Just the rattle of the aspen leaves as the wind picks up.
The roar of a plane overhead? Not at all. You will have
heard the distinctive booming, as opposed to the mewing call,
of the giant buzzard which nests in and around Gatwick.
The incessant electric drill? Sheep farmer more like,
lovingly shearing his flock of Herdwick, ideal beasts
for grazing on the gentle slopes of Happy Valley.
A loud cacophony of foreign voices? Seasonal immigrant
labourers toiling happily in a distant asparagus field.

'Well, that's enough of me rambling on. Now it's your turn.
I sincerely hope you have enjoyed our little walk, and if you wish
to continue on the nature trail, follow the edge of the field to the bottom
of the valley and through the kissing gate until you reach the woodland.
Goodbye.' **Stop**.

'And . . . Action!'

Afternoon tea on the lawn of the White House
when, uninvited, a truck with nobody
at the wheel crashes through the railings
and hurtles towards the Rose Garden.

Sandwiches and senators are scattered
in the skidding, zigzaggy onslaught.
Colonels scream, tyres squeal,
canapés squashed beneath the wheel.

Out of control, the truck is heading
straight towards the President.
No one moves. Slow motion now,
as in a dream. He turns to face it.

Screech. Smash. Smithereens.
Then silence. Grinning, he removes
a windshield wiper from his hair,
straightens his tie, puffs out his chest.

Turning to camera, he holds up a fist,
then saunters to the helipad. On cue,
the band strikes up, the crowd begins to clap.
'Cut,' shouts the director. 'It's a wrap.'

The Pips

From the beginning of March 2020, the Today *programme on BBC Radio 4, in an effort to publicise shows that had been cancelled owing to lockdown, featured some of the actors and musicians performing live to give a flavour of what audiences had missed. Unfortunately, coming at the end of the programme, it was always a race against time. And time inevitably won.*

Watching the film and the credits roll two minutes in
Watching the play and the curtain comes down as soon as the actors begin

Pip . . .

The pianist sits at the keyboard, the singer clears her throat
Cue pips to invade the studio at the sound of the opening note

Pip . . .

The folk singer with a backlog of songs from long ago
The up-and-coming cellist has hardly flexed her bow
That aria from an opera, the one in which she died.
The jazz trumpeter is muted, before he hits his stride

Pip . . .

What the world needs now is news, not arias or the blues
Not sonatas or soliloquies, but headlines and the news
Not banter or poetry, this is not the time to amuse
Cue pips to invade the studio, what the world needs now is news

Pip . . .

Fast-forward the headlines, we're all craving for a fix
Of Covid, Boris, Trump, all thrown into the mix

Pip . . .

The show must go on, but sadly not on here
The pips are on their way, news addicts have no fear

PIP.

Bad Timing

Oh, what dreadful timing, it couldn't have been worse
For that long-awaited, ground-breaking volume of verse

Neat, intriguing title, warm and welcoming cover
Author smiling on the back, then *Whoosh* it's all over

Your publisher hired a publicist to titillate the press
A review already promised in the *TLS*, no less

Fingers crossed for Waterstones and a window display
The launch in Covent Garden, and the following day

A signing at Harrods (high on your bucket list)
Practising your signature, you almost sprained your wrist

Then all aboard the reading circuit (50 mins plus Q&A)
Dropping by at bookstores and libraries on the way

A choice of literary festivals, Cheltenham, Hay-on-Wye
Chats on local radio, and hopefully on Sky

But what untimely timing, how could anybody guess
Your career as a poet would last an hour or less?

A laureate in the making, surely next in line for the crown
Had your book not been released, the day the world shut down.

When It's Over

What will we have learned from stillness and silence?
From sharing, not taking? Waiting, not pushing?
Whispering, not shouting? Dawdling, not rushing?
When life is back to normal and the hugging is over
Will we look beyond ourselves and help the Earth recover?

This morning, the only cloud.
On the horizon is a cloud.

Without fear of intrusion,
it drifts above, full of itself.

The sky, has it had a facial?
Its skin positively glows.

Is it a bird? Is it a plane?
Superman? No, just a bird.

And on a branch, another is singing.
The purity of the note!

No need today to clear its throat.
If trees could smile, this one surely would.

Imprisoned for our sins,
is now the time to question why?

When it's over, what lessons?
Ask the tree, the bird and the sky.

Eternity, same old

Inevitably, a few of the gods grew bored with eternity.
Same old thing, day after day, year after year, century
after century, aeon after aeon, etcetera after etcetera.

Of course, there were the fun times. When not cavorting
and carousing, devising new ways of keeping the humans
anxious and fearful. Like whipping up thunderstorms,

spinning tornadoes, burping volcanoes, spewing tsunamis,
cooking up new recipes for plagues. And the old favourites,
the tried-and-trusted famine and war. Happy days.

But the days seemed to be endless. Which they were.
Melt a few more ice caps? Yawn. Throw a few more
logs on the bush fire? Yawn, yawn. Up to here.

The gods had had it up to here. Until one yawny,
heavy-lidded morning, one of them had a brainwave.
'Just for a change,' she said, 'just for a giggle,

let's make the poor sods happy. For one day only.
We'll call it Happy Humans Day.' The other gods
looked up from their carousing and cavorting.

'For instance, volcanoes could spout wisdom.'
'Plagues could eat themselves,' suggested another,
'Gentle tsunamis deliver gifts of gold,' said another.

'No more killing or cruelty, famine or disease.'
Excited now, the gods competed to think up clever ways
of bringing instant happiness to 7.7 billion people.

Some ideas were ingenious, as you'd expect,
while others were just silly, but the brainstorming
sessions were great fun while they lasted.

Of course, they never got around to actually *doing*
anything, just thinking about it, but it took their minds
off things for a few centuries or so.

By which time the gods had grown bored again
and completely forgotten the point of the exercise.
One whistled up an avalanche, another crashed a train.

One brought down the internet, another a plane.
One hawked and spat a deadly virus. One yawned,
and so did another. And so on, and so on. Etcetera, etcetera, etcetera.

Attic Salt

A granma is an anagram of anagram. (Sorry pan rag)

Baby's first words *'No comment'* set alarm bells ringing

Collisions are always first to arrive at the scene

Dog-eat-dog world? Definitely, and vice versa

Echoes thrill to the sound of their own voices . . . voices . . . voices

Flat-Earthers finally concede they were wrong. The Earth is pear-shaped

God-fearing atheists hedge their bets. Gambling topiarists bet their hedges

Hyenas are not afraid to laugh at themselves

Isthmuses are the bane of lisping oceanographers

Jiu-jitsu is not for the ticklish

Knives, even the sharpest, rarely cut through red tape

Late-comers are always dead on time for their own funerals

Matadors matter less today than yesterday. Olé

Nasal floss, unlike candy floss, never caught on

Oval eggs were a joy to lay after all those square ones

Peer pressure prevents possibility of Parliamentary reform

Quibbling and Squabbling, two villages in Devon best avoided

Rear-view mirrors are a boon to upskirters and bottom-watchers

Shooting stars. A spaceman's hobby that should be banned

Tipping the executioner is frowned upon in Texas

Underdeveloped countries may beg to differ

Vox pop? No word for it in North Korean

Wrestlers when wrestled to the ground wrestle with the idea of wretirement

X-ray selfies? Not on Tinder, yet

You. Yes, you. You are amazing! Attractive and intelligent. I am in awe*

Zen, zinc, zeitgeist, zero, zucchini, zodiac, zip, zigzag, zombie. Enough zed

* *A ploy often used in the poetry trade to retain a reader's interest.*

Creeping Up on Poetry

Creep up on poetry while she's feeding the ducks.
Don't startle her, though, you might end up in the water.
And talking of being out of your depth, if she invites you
to a book launch, don't go. The sight of a slim volume
sliding down a slipway into the river may cause queasiness.

If it is raining heavily at the bus stop,
don't ask poetry if you could share her umbrella,
you will end up paying her fare and carrying her bags.
Rather, pretend you enjoy getting soaked.
Look up into the sky, open your arms and sing.

If poetry should lose patience and scream at you,
threaten to take up gaming and accountancy.
And remember, that poem you are about to write
has already been written, many times over.
But carry on, fresh pair of eyes, ears and all that.

If poetry puts the phone down on you,
wash your hands, count to ten and then ring back.
'Hello, you have reached poetry. We are sorry
but there is nobody here at the moment.'
Odd. Isn't that your voice on the answerphone?

Sidle up to poetry while she is on the platform
checking the Underground map. When she
has finished, introduce yourself and amuse her
with stories of accountancy, ducks, book launches,
and that poem you are about to write.

If she runs up the escalator, don't be tempted
to follow. You have missed your chance.
Instead, go home and begin writing that poem
that has already been written many times over.
Fresh pair of eyes, ears and all that.

The New One

I really enjoyed being with the last one.
It was a long, intense relationship
and I didn't want it to end. But end it did.

And the one before? Difficult at times.
So much so, I thought about giving up
and walking away. Glad now I didn't.

And the first. Who can forget the first?
My life changed for ever. What I lacked in
technique, I made up for in passion.

So many since. Some funny,
others serious and questioning.
Such intensity while they lasted.

And now that I've found a new one,
already I can feel the reassuring promise
of triplets and good rhymes ahead.

The poet as polygamist.
Same church, same vow, new bride.

'Writing another poem is like polygamy'
– Martin Hall

A Labour of Love

Conceived? Possibly at home, or in the park.
Walking the dog perhaps? Even a crowded pub.
The library, its silence rarely failing to arouse.

A home birth preferably, just the two of you.
Although coffee bar or crowded train if needs must.
If it's on its way, so be it. Get it down.

You've done the hard labour, now for the easy part.
Clean with loving care then hold up for all to see.
Feel justly proud. Looks like you.

The poet as gynaecologist.
Another poem born, screaming for attention.

The Poem you are about to Read has not yet been Written

The poem you are about to read has not yet been written.
Looks can be deceptive. Ignore the shape on the page,
the arrangement of the lines to form stanzas.
You could be forgiven for thinking it is the real McCoy.

The fact that it appears confidently in a book of verse
might lead you to believe that it is a poem fully formed,
but you would be wrong. It is not even a work in progress,
merely the ghost of an idea come to visit one night.

Was it Auden or Robert Frost who said you should never
waste a good title? Whoever it was, they were right.

Out of My Depth in Language

Early dawn, and on the point of giving up
I see coastal lights, take a deep breath and strike out.

Scared of heights, the moon still clings to the sky.
But stars, having lost interest, are calling it a day.

Beneath, fish wriggle through nets
like mischievous noughts and crosses.

On the seabed, a book of poems by Stevie Smith
(open at page 303) lies half buried.

* * *

Land is within sight but I hesitate. Dive,
rescue the book, and swim towards the shore.
It is further away than I thought. Much further.

What they saw, hours later, those stretched out
on the sand, or dozing in deckchairs,
was a man far out at sea waving a book.

For him the shore was always out of reach
and he never made it. Like the man
in the poem, in the book, on the beach.

The Land of Lost Tongues

(Manx Gaelic: The Celtic dialect of the Isle of Man became extinct in 1974 with the death of the last native speaker.)

An old man walks into a corner shop and asks
in perfect Manx for a packet of chewing gum,
a tube of glue, and a bottle of orange juice.
The young lad behind the counter says, 'Pardon?'

Gumless, glueless and juiceless, the old man
returns home to find his wife collapsed
on the kitchen floor. He telephones for an
ambulance, but the girl in emergency services,
being from Manchester, says, 'Pardon?'

The old man rushes out into the busy street
and in pure Manx Gaelic appeals for help
to passers-by, who either nod sympathetically,
give directions to the ferry, or say, 'Pardon?'

The old woman dies. The old man is struck dumb,
and Manx Gaelic, having nobody to talk to,
sets off in search of the Land of Lost Tongues
as fast as his three legs can carry him.

Violin Left on Train

I'm totally devastated
I left my violin on the train
It feels like losing a limb
and I suffer unbearable pain

Tired after a busy day
recording Rimsky-Korsakov
I boarded the train at Victoria
and must have nodded off

When we stopped at Orpington
I rushed off half awake
And only as the doors banged shut
did I realise my mistake.

By the way, I also left a baby
up there on the luggage rack
So, if you should come across it
we'd love to have her back.

The Graveyard Slot

(A poet's nightmare)

Imagine a violinist without a violin
standing on stage wondering how to begin.
Could mime, of course, a silent recital,
but you'd feel let down, the music is vital.
Well, I'm in the same boat, in a similar plight,
I'm a poet without a poem to recite.
And so, as an aide-memoire, on reaching the venue
I scribbled some notes on the back of a menu.

Now this suddenly feels like the graveyard slot
no fee, no poems, and a 5-minute spot
between the comedian and the burlesque dancer.
My agent's got a lot to answer . . .
For . . . to be honest, although a 5-minute spot
compared to eternity may not seem a lot.
Time is a bucket, lowered s-l-o-w-l-y into a well,
and the well is bottomless, as far as I can tell.

(*Checks watch*.) Still 4 and a half minutes yet to fill,
the prospect of which makes me feel ill.
You wonder why? Well, let me explain . . .
I left all my poems behind on the train.
That's why I'm nervous and look a bit harassed,
but it's a long story and I'm slightly embarrassed.
Trouble is, I never learned them by heart
and at my age it's far too late to start.

The spoken word, rap and grime
I leave to the kids, I don't have the time.
So, without my book, and words on the page
I'm a fish out of water up here on the stage.
Paralysed by the crowd's puzzled gaze,
'The eyes have it,' as the Speaker says.
I'm little more than a figure of speech,
as nervous as a nun on a nudist beach.

3 minutes to go, which is still a long time
and not easy to find that perfect rhyme.
(Though, to be honest, poems don't have to.
They can just be a jumble of words thrown together for the reader,
or in your case, the listener, to make sense of.)
But I prefer rhyme, it's my stock in trade.
If it don't make music, it don't make the grade.
As T. S. Eliot confided as we cruised down the street,
'Choose words that sing and are light on their feet.'

Did I tell you I left my poems on the train?
Of course I did, but I'll tell you again.
Only halfway through and I'm losing the plot,
dying a death in the graveyard slot.
I was coming here on the Tube, thinking about the show,
about which poems to read and where they go,
rearranging them in my loose-leaf folder,
when a lady got on, eighty, maybe older,

so, I stood up and said, 'Take the weight off your feet,'
when this guy pushes in and grabs the seat.
'You bastard,' I said. 'Not you, madam, him.'
At which he stood up and kneed me in the nuts.

(I know that doesn't rhyme, but as I pointed out earlier
poems don't have to. They can just be a jumble of words
thrown together for the listener, or in your case,
the reader, to make sense of.)

I don't think I can keep up the pretence any more,
my brain's going numb and my throat's getting sore.
I feel like an actor without a script . . .
Anyway, this guy on the train, he really flipped,
hit me round the head, with my folder in fact,
I was lucky to get out at the next station intact.
But what bugs me, what really makes me sick,
is that right now he'll be in, like, Hackney Wick,

or Brighton at a poetry slam, my folder in hand,
reading poems he doesn't understand.
But the audience will, and how they'll applaud,
not knowing he's a seat-snatcher, a thief and a fraud.
And next he'll be on YouTube and all over Twitter,
not that I'm jealous, of course, or bitter,
but come on, be honest, how would you feel
if someone nicked your poems and got a publishing deal?

But, stuff happens, and life goes on,
so, you'll be glad to hear that I'm almost done.
And things aren't always as bad as they seem,
maybe I'll wake up, and it was only a dream
about the ghost of a violinist unable to play
and that of a poet with nothing to say.

Five seconds more and I'm off like a shot . . .
Free at last from the graveyard slot
. . . 3 . . . 2 . . . 1 . . . Goodnight!

Violin Left on Train (Part Two)

Thank you for returning the baby
Just look at the smile on her face
Lying there all warm and cosy
Tucked up in my violin case

But at the risk of sounding churlish
After you've been so honest and kind
Though it's nice to have the baby back
It's the violin that I'm desperate to find

I'm at the Albert Hall tomorrow
Playing an early Mendelssohn piece
So please go home and fetch it
Or I'm going to fetch the police

What do you mean, you're sorry?
And of course, I'm making a fuss!
How could anybody be so stupid
As to leave a violin behind on a bus!

Quodlibets

Zzzzzzzzzz . . . Wake up! Wake up! You're on first

Yesterday woke up this morning thinking it was today. Phew! Back to sleep

Xenophile or xenophobe? Xeno is well past caring

Windfalls from hurricanes are welcomed by wind farmers

Vlad the Impala, infamous name, the antelope hangs its antlers in shame

Underwater lakes, not bubbling, but sobbing in eternal darkness

Trans-Iberian Railway is Spain's gift to non-binary travellers

Shadows of the deceased can be purchased on the dark web

Rasputin begat Putin. No disputin

'Quornhub': Sexy adult fun for vegetarians

Pubism as an art movement, although fun, was short-lived

Osteopaths are good to walk along if you have back pain

Nightmares, nervous on opening nights, fidget and fluff their lines

Mona Lisa smiled when Leonardo said, 'OK, you can go to the toilet now'

Lizards, legless on lager, lie low in the lounge of the Chameleon Club

Kleptomaniacs can't help helping themselves

'*Je ne sais* quoit,' whooped the hoop, looping the loop

Instant gratification takes too long for some people

Hangover? The sediment in alcohol's poisoned chalice

Gastronomers scan the heavens in search of Michelin stars

Fast food is fine if you are fasting

'Eureka!' sighed Archimedes as she climbed into the bath with him

Dust is the carpet of the contented

Cocktail party. Waiting ages for a bouche, then three come along at once

Balls of string theory are notoriously difficult to unravel

Amen. At the end. Always and for ever. Amen.

Where Babies Come From

As the subject was never mentioned at home,
I have an elderly Irish Christian Brother to thank
for teaching me all I would need to know about sex.
Brother Nolan was my form master at junior school,
and creeping up behind me one morning in his soft Irish
brogues, asked if I was ever troubled by 'thoughts'.

'Not that I know of, sir.' Himself insisted. 'Dark thoughts.
Is there anything you want to know about . . . sex?'
To be honest, there wasn't, but not to appear churlish,
I stammered, 'Where do babies come from?'
He took a long, reflective drag on a stick of chalk
then walked away. Had I gone too far, I wondered?

Part of his duties involved running the stock room
and doling out sports gear, exercise books, ink,
board dusters and boxes of chalk, etc. Yes, chalk.
Like putting Billy Bunter in charge of the tuck shop.
As requested, I turned up there next morning
and knocked nervously on the door.

He opened it, and first checking the corridor was clear,
beckoned me in. Drawing closer, Nolan whispered,
'You'll find the answer to your question
under that box of pencils by the window.
Read it carefully, and I'll be back in forty minutes.'
He then disappeared, locking the door behind him.

Of course, being ten years old, I was more interested
in the contents of the stock room than in the words
of wisdom that were destined to change my life.
So, I tried on a first-team rugby shirt, puffed on my first
piece of chalk, got a finger stuck in a test tube,
and measured my head with a large, wooden compass.

Eventually I read the note, which said simply,
'The baby is a seed.' 'If that's true,' I thought, 'then why
aren't we all flowers?' As the bell rang for the end of playtime
he unlocked the door and led me down the corridor.
'From now you'll not be troubled by any more "thoughts",
but say your prayers every night, just to be on the safe side.'

Creative Waiting

('Poetry writing workshop today at 16.00 in the library. All welcome.')

15.40
The August sun streaming in,
so quiet you can hear the wagtails
hopping across the manicured lawns.

15.50
As the newly appointed Poet-in-Residence
at Crannoch Castle, I am keen to spread the word
and show how poetry can inspire and change lives.

16.00
My first creative-writing workshop will begin
any minute now, and I can sense the impatience
of pencils and paper laid out on the long oak table.

16.10
Those who can afford to join this exclusive club
come mainly from the USA. Bankers and top execs
who love their golf, their riding and their shooting.

16.20
It is a lovely day for golf, riding and shooting.
Cycling perhaps to the beach at Dornoch
or simply walking around the vast estate.

16.30
Perhaps, because of their busy schedules,
and jetlag, members have lost track of time?
Perhaps they are waiting in another library?

16.40
Perhaps, in preparation for the session,
they have been studying my collected poems,
and over-awed, lack the confidence to attend?

16.50
I could go in search of them, I suppose?
Trouble is, they might turn up here and wonder
where the tutor is. Imagine their disappointment.

17.00
Time's up. Rejected, the poet-in-reticence
wipes away a tear for the sonnets unborn.
Suddenly, a knock at the door. 'Come in.'

* * *

17.30
The cleaner's name is Marta Zámborová
from Sarajevo, whose command of English
is not perfect but who loves poetry.

22.45
So far this evening, Marta has not only written
three sonnets, four villanelles, and an epithalamium
but has introduced me to several Slavic verse forms.

00.00
It is beautiful down here by the loch.
Moonlight, and the gentle lapping of the water.
'What is *reticence*?' she asks, removing my hand.

Global Haggis Day

They're scoffing haggis in Sydney while surfing on Bondi Beach
In Reykjavik they like it thick, lots of vodka within reach

A million clicking chopsticks mix haggis with rice in China
Japanese guzzling sushi-haggis agree there's nothing finer

In Hyderabad, they all go mad for sporran-shaped chapatis
Stuffed with curried haggis, hot chilli, neaps and tatties

In the Middle East they love to feast on haggis without meat
With peaches, dates and honey, and custard, hot and sweet

On every Texan barbecue a haggis-burger sits
(Think melted cheese with black-eyed peas, curly fries and grits)

Spanish mums add saffron to make it nice and yeller
'Olé!' they shout when they bring it out . . . 'Viva la haggis paella!'

I migliori ristorante serve haggis-filled ravioli
His Holiness in Rome has blessed our dish and made it holy

In every four-star restaurant and every greasy spoon,
Haggis is the plat du jour, so the world is over the moon

So, with poems and songs and funny turns
We celebrate auld Robbie Burns
And in doing so, we make a wish:
'Long live our nation, and our dish.'

The View

It isn't easy being a view.
The weight of expectation.
All it needs is a downpour or a heavy mist
and I'm sniffed at. Written off.

On a clear day, though, I can lie back
and bask in the warm admiration
that flows towards me. I pose.
I am the very model of a landscape.

Welcome. Relax and sit awhile.
And remember, what you see is the view
but what the view sees is *you*.
So, Big Smile!

The Puzzle Tree

If I were born again as a tree,
Which one would I choose to be?

Poplars are popular, and Firs first class
Ash cut a dash, and a Silver Birch
is worth the search any day

A Willow, its branches sweeping low
like a ballerina taking a bow
can take the breath away

Pine trees seem to own the land
on which they stand
Catch a falling cone and make a wish

The mighty Oak that towers above
the rest, has stood the test of time
What's not to love?

How the Aspen gently quivers when the wind
is in its sails. The Rowan uses magic
when spinning its dark tales

Conference, Bramley, Granny Smith,
Apple and Pear trees take some beating
Each fall, their gifts, ours for the eating

Horse Chestnuts have the best nuts
(although not to be eaten). Playing conkers
at school I couldn't be beaten

While the Holly has more thorns, Hawthorns
have much to be admired, and I'm fired
by the sight of a flowering Cherry

Towering Christmas trees make me merry
While Hornbeams, by babbling streams
provide a backdrop to restful dreams

If I were born again as a tree,
Which one would I choose to be?

Ash and Elm, I have watched them grow
Linden, Larch, they come and go
Blackthorn, Beech and Sycamore too
(I'm getting old. Now there's the clue.)

Let's Hear It for Poetry

Let's hear it for poetry
The learning and the writing of it
The reading and the telling

For who led us there
Parents, friends, lovers, teachers
The loan of a book, the ticket for a gig

A big hand for landscape
First frost of winter, full moon and rainbows
The heart that leaps, the eyes that behold

For suburbia. Mown lawns
And wisteria, pink and fully blown
Let us celebrate the desire to escape

Thumbs up for the city. Its excitement
And excesses. The late hours it keeps
The history beneath its feet

Three cheers for the crowded room
Take the words by the hand
Let them lead you in the dance

Let us celebrate the birth of the poem
The need to question, to inspire and create.
Let us count the ways. Let us celebrate.

Stuffed

On the bookshelf, an A–Z of forgotten poets.
'O'er long and shadeless days, the tinkling silence thrills.'
I could bring that back from the dead. Ditch the 'O'er'
then, '*something* hills'? Or possibly, '*something* daffodils'?

'Safe at last, she begins to unpick the stitches.'
I'll have that. Of a flag perhaps? And this:
'The armed raven bestrides the smouldering nest.'
Armed raven? Weird, but may lead somewhere.

The poet as taxidermist.
Stuffing the flaccid carcass of stillborn poems.

The Failed Taxidermist

Each night in my attic room
I chat to Coleridge via Zoom
And long for days when I'm allowed,
To wander lonely in a crowd.

Among the sheep who gently graze,
Where, through long and shadeless days
And the tinkling silence thrills,
I walk among the daffodils.

The above, sadly, is all that remains
of a long poem that took ages to write.
To craft it carefully I took great pains
Redrafted, revised throughout the night.

(Its conceit was the intrusion of modern tech
upon nature, with reference to the Lyrical Ballads,
set against a dark background of the pandemic.)

But this morning it showed its true face
Gurning, sneering up at me
For although my heart was in the right place
The words were not, would never be.

Narrator's Disease

Thursday knew it was going to be a red-letter day.
The sense of its own importance shook Bernard
by the shoulder as he lay in bed trying to hitch a lift
from passing dream pantechnicons. Wondering
what was so special about red letters, he lowered
a weary thumb and dragged himself out of bed.

His wife, Pamela (or Pam, for short), was already up and doing.
The sound of muesli drifted up from the kitchen,
and he could almost imagine the shape of the croissants
and picture the aroma of freshly ground coffee.
Following a quick shower in the room where the shower was,
he dressed and went downstairs, Thursday not far behind.

'*More coffee?*' asked his wife, Pamela (or Pam, for short).
'**No thanks,**' said Bernard. '**What with the price of avocados
and the rise of populism in certain parts of Europe,
it's a wonder anybody can.**' The silence that followed
stretched across the table between them like Ayers Rock
covered in bacon fat. '*Pardon?*'

'**I said the silence that followed stretched across the table
between them like Ayers Rock covered . . .**' Pam interrupted,
'*You know what day it is today, don't you?*'
Bernard looked over her shoulder towards the window,
where Thursday was standing, its name emblazoned
on its T-shirt. '**Thursday?**' '*Correct. And that means?*'

'My meeting.' *'Who with?'* **'Doctor Bell.'** *'What time?'*
'3.20 this afternoon.' *'Where?'* **'Davidson Street.'**
'What number?' **'28.'** Pamela gently took her hand in his.
'You've a memory like a neutered budgie sometimes,
so just once more to be on the safe side?'
'4 o'clock, 32 Hollandaise Avenue, Doctor Tourette.'

Bernard walked along Harley Street until he reached
number 320, and looked up at the imposing building
the way a Buddhist mouse might behold a giant
mousetrap sculpted out of cheese. He took the steps
two at a time, before replacing them carefully
and ringing the bell marked 'Bell'. ***'Who is that?'***

said what could only be described as a voice.
'Hello, I'm here to see the doctor.' *'Name?'*
'Bell, I think it is.' *'No, your name.'* **'Oh, Ashcroft,
Bernard Ashcroft.'** ***'Come in, Mr Ashcroft,
Mr Bell is expecting you.'*** Expecting me to what?
thought Bernard as he hurried into the lift.

Mr Bell was wearing a dark grey suit with a red shirt.
Tall, thin and balding, with a few straggles of hair
limping forlornly across his scalp like frayed tightropes.
Early fifties, I'd say. *'Forty-five,'* corrected the doctor.
*'I'm forty-five, and I don't much care for the image
of the frayed tightropes. And the shirt is pink.*

'I'm afraid you have a serious medical condition.'
The doctor had hit the nail right on the head.
'As you say, I've hit the nail right on the head.'
'Did I say that? I thought I only thought it.'
*'No, you said it out loud. And that's your problem.
The inability to keep your thoughts to yourself.*

'Narrator's Disease, that's what we in the trade call it.
Otherwise known as Third Person Syndrome.
A phobia in which the real world is seen purely in terms
of a story in which the narrator is a passive observer.'
Doctor Bell took a crisp linen handkerchief from his
trouser pocket and . . . *'Do shut up!'* **'Sorry.'**

'Is there a cure, Doctor?' *'As far as the eye can see,*
you have two options. Either carry on as you are,
making not only your own life a misery but the lives
of those around you, or choose the second option.'
'Which is?' *'The operation option.'* **'Brain surgery?'**
'Yes, a new procedure I have recently perfected.'

'Is it dangerous?' *'I don't know, I've yet to try it*
on a human being.' **'You want me to be a guinea pig?'**
'No, I want you to be a human being, I'm up to here
with guinea pigs.' **'You've operated successfully**
on animals then?' *'Frequently. How many rabbits*
do you see wandering around telling stories?'

'But I'm not a rabbit, am I? Or a guinea pig, or a chimp?
I'm a man, with free will and a soul. I'm an amazing
piece of biological engineering. Blood goes round
and stuff comes out. I can sing, dance and do sums.
Not only can I make love, but I can cook steak au poivre
with pommes dauphinoise and a side salad on the side.'

'Enough prevarication, Bernard! You have two choices
to consider. Number one, a life of disappointment
caused by the failure of the real you to live up
to the fictional character you create for yourself.
Number two, my preferred option, say the word
and in two ticks I'll have you up on the slab,
and your head split open like a ripe watermelon.'

'Here's your breakfast, love. Fresh instant coffee
and croissants. You've been through hell and back.'
'There were people in hospital worse off than me.'
'But you're home now and every cloud has a silver lining.'
'And every bandage dreams of being the Shroud of Turin.'
'Very true. Was that the doorbell?'

'A visitor for you, Bernard. I'll go and put the kettle on.'
'I didn't expect to see you again, Doctor Bell.'
'I came to apologise for putting you under pressure.
It was unethical of me, causing you to panic like that.'
'It wasn't your fault. You weren't to know the phobia
that made me run downstairs and across the street.'

'Watermelons? Of course, so you didn't see the pantechnicon?'
'No, too busy worrying about hospitals and operations.'
'And the next thing, you're in hospital having an operation?'
'Yes. Thanks for calling an ambulance, by the way.'
'The least I could do, being a trained surgeon, that is.
On the plus side, no recurrence of the dreaded Narrator's?'

Some weeks later Bernard Ashcroft was limping out
of Westminster Hospital, his leg in a fresh plaster cast,
when who should he see on the steps of the Odeon
but Doctor Bell and his wife, Pamela (or Pam for short).
They were in a deep, passionate embrace, oblivious
to the comings and goings of the cinema-comers and goers.

You can imagine the pain, the utter confusion.
Suddenly, his world turned upside out and inside down.
As fast as his cast would carry him, he advanced on them,
screaming, **'Hands off my wife, you bastard, or I shall . . .'**
When the couple turned in alarm to confront him
he realised they were complete strangers.

'Hardly strangers,' said the lady, 'This is my fiancé.'
'*And this is my fiancée,*' added the gentleman, adding an *e*.
To hide his withering shame and embarrassment
Bernard darted into the cinema just in time to catch
the closing credits of the film: *Narrator's Disease*,
starring Bernard Ashcroft, Dr Bell and Pamela (or Pam for short).

The End

Tensions

Why is the past tense?
All that unfinished business
And no going back

*

Why is the present tense?
Having to make it all up
As it goes along

*

Why is the future tense?
The weight of expectation
And time running out

A Silence Crying Out for Attention

The women went out

leaving a silence

so palpable

you could count the s y ll a bles

Safe at last the men began to unpick the stitches

before doing those jobs

only grown men can do:

Rearranging

the ripe figs in the bowl

Sanitising the remote

Disarming the raven.

(Conspicuous by its absence, the meaning slips through a gap in the void.)

Taking advantage of the hiatus

I turn to the writer:

'Where are you going with this?'

Too late!

I am

over

the page

and

away.............

And You Are?

And you are?
I am the one who is always first in the queue, but you never let me in.

And you are?
I am a friend of the guy whose friend used to be the guy on the door.

And you are?
I am the apple of my mother's eye, the answer to a maiden's prayer.

And you are?
I am the owner. Your employer. No, I don't have any ID.

And you are?
I am the woman who sleeps in the car park above Waitrose.

And you are?
I am the writer who escaped from the poem over the page.

And you are?
I am the stripper, and it's bloody cold out here.

And you are?
I have no idea. I was hoping someone inside could tell me.

And you are?
I am the one who is always last in the queue. Any queue. Always last.

Another Long Queue

I do as I'm told
and join the queue.
It is a long queue.

We move up slowly
and in silence.
I don't have time for this.

'What are we queuing for?'
I ask the lady in front.
'To join another queue.'

'This is stupid,' I say.
'I don't have time for this,
I'm leaving.'

She points to another long line.
'Then you must join
that queue over there.'

I do as I'm told
and join this queue over here.
It is a long queue.

We move up slowly
and in silence.
I don't have time for this.

Torchlight Procession

Out walking along the cliff top early one evening
I caught up with a large group treading the same path.
In need of company and small talk, I tagged along.
Good company they were not.

Instead, there was a sense of desperation
as they hurried on, grim-faced and solemn
like mourners in search of a lost coffin.
Too late to turn back, I was too tired to overtake.

It was getting cold and dark. Torches were produced
and light shone on the path, into the bushes,
and on the grass leading to the cliff edge.
Somebody called my name. 'Yes,' I replied wearily.

The man ahead of me stopped and directed
the beam into my face. 'It's you, isn't it? It's you?'
'Er, yes. Why?' The group fell silent and turned.
'Call off the search,' he shouted, 'I've found him.'

Warning Signs

Halfway through the book before realising you have read it

Having one for the road as soon as you get home

How did my jeans get into the dishwasher?

Ordering dim sum in your local Italian

Time to hit the road? You stumble, hit the road.

Having nightmares about winning the lottery

Pre-traumatic stress. No traumas, no excuses

This can't be my memory, I wasn't even born then

Same old question, whose brain have you got this time?

Worry they will talk about you once you have left the room

Autumn? But we've only just had winter

Paying for coffee with a Senior Railcard

'Hail Mary, full of grace' . . . What comes next?

Worry the room will talk about you once they have left

Why do they keep changing the names of the roads?

It's written down somewhere, but where?

Having one for the road as soon as you get up

Putting it back on the shelf, you recognise your name on the cover.

Anybody There?

There are times when I feel I'm not real
Not made out of flesh, but thin air
Surrounded by friends who don't notice
Listen, or let alone care.

When I told my therapist this morning
She turned and said, 'Anybody there?'

In My Corner

Thank you for the brainwashing,
which seems to have worked. No disasters,
touch wood. Fingers crossed, so far so good.

No family trauma, the occasional scare.
To keep them safe I pay my dues,
help fill the pews and chance a prayer.

Of course, from time to time I fail. Sin?
We had some good times you and I, until
that spoilsport *Conscience* reined me in.

Some scoff and jeer. Cloud cuckoo land.
It's all mumbo-jumbo. Just a con.
Who knows? Against the odds we soldier on.

People cleverer than me think I'm naïve.
That God is dead, that when it ends, it ends.
I fight my corner armed with guilt and doubt.

And so, when it's time for me to leave,
Religion, you'd better believe, you owe me.
So, be there, and be sure to hang about.

Last Times

The last time I saw a quokka on Rottnest Island
off the coast of Perth in Western Australia
I didn't know it would be the last time.
If I had, would I have looked more closely?
Stayed longer, taken more photographs?
Although, as I recall, I didn't take any.

The last time I saw my father, he was sitting up
in bed in Walton Hospital, Liverpool,
trying to look cheerful after a second heart attack.
I didn't know it would be the last time,
although I rather suspect that he did,
resolute in the pretence that big dockers don't cry.

The last verse, the last round of drinks,
the last bus home, we see them come and go,
but when Last Time jumps the queue, watch out.
Our not knowing only adding to the poignancy.
That stroking of the cat, that sighting of a bird.
There is a first time for everything, and a last.

Envoi

As was his custom, the author poured himself
a large scotch to celebrate the birth of a new poem.
Then, fearing it might be the last time,
hastily and clumsily, he poured himself another.

Chained to the Past

'It's like being chained to some dead actress.'
– LeRoi Jones

Not dead so much as failed.
Her career had never taken off,
and on those walks across the common
on unseasonably warm February afternoons,
she would complain endlessly.

About the duplicity of fellow actors,
the greed of agents, the prejudice and bias
of self-serving directors. I point out the daffodils,
a sprinkling of snowdrops. Sexual harassment.
The same stories over and over.

Though bare of leaves, the gnarled beauty
of the sycamore. Dressing-room rituals in theatres
I have never visited, nor are likely to.
'Look, a chaffinch.' Plays I have no wish to see,
starring actors I have never heard of. Or will.

On some days I am tempted to loosen the chains
and set her free. Bid her run and run
into the imaginary past she so desired,
returning with Oscars, Baftas and bouquets
clutched to her bosom. But she won't.

On other days I am tempted to loosen the chains
and set myself free. Bid myself run and run
into the real and recent past, but I can't
and never will. 'Too early for a chaffinch,' she says,
before turning me round and wheeling me home.

Bad Clowns

(i)

'Audiences I can't abide

Than enter the ring I'd rather hide

After an hour the greasepaint stinks

The strongman's not as strong as he thinks

I sneeze when the sawdust gets up my nose

The acrobats never change their clothes

Children annoy me, no circus will employ me

I don't know why,' said Cantankerous the Clown.

(ii)

'I can be a bit naughty and my jokes can be blue

But there's sawdust in my blood,

I'm a showman through and through

A roll of drums as I climb on the chair

My trousers fall down and my bottom is bare

But people know it's rude to stare

So why am I always run out of town?

I don't understand it,' said Flasher the Clown.

(iii)

'In the Big Top when the lights are low

I like to creep between each row, of children,

And without a sound, spread the cobwebs all around

Then my spiders I introduce, wish them well and set them loose

You can imagine the kids, how they scream and shout

Until the band strikes up and drowns them out

At the end of the season I've been told to go

Why kiddies don't like me I'll never know,'

Said Kreepy the Klown.

(iv)

'I can do cartwheels way up on the high wire

My juggling is faultless, I'm annoyed

Ride the backs of two tigers while eating fire

So why am I still unemployed?

I'm no ignoramus, so why aren't I famous?

I should be the toast of the town

Although performers admire me, no circus will hire me

I don't understand it,' said Covid the Clown.

My Night with Laura Kuenssberg

It was more than a night, actually,
but days and nights, for it was a long journey
in a windowless wagon on a crowded train.
Just us and the child. Yours, I supposed,
although it might have been your little sister.

As you slept, I tried to imagine the nightmares
besetting you, Big Ben, the door of Number Ten,
a youth gurning in the background. And the rain,
light at first, turning heavy later in the day,
with the promise of sunshine by the weekend.

On arrival, I wished you well, but wanted nothing
in return. Saving you was enough. And your name.
Like Tomasz Schafernaker, hard to say, difficult
to spell. Please, no more running away. Without you,
Politics and Weather would never be the same.

Villanelle

An actress who is always in the news
Her name is Villanelle
(And she sticks up for the Blues)

If I had to be exterminated, I would choose
this assassin who casts a spell
An actress who is always in the news

The star of *Killing Eve*, she gets the best reviews
(Oh, Sandra Oh, it must be hell!)
Though it's a game that neither of you lose

A Scouser whom no one can accuse
of being a big 'ead. She's nice, you can tell
Otherwise why stick up for the Blues?

I tried to write a villanelle
(But like Everton, haven't done too well)
For an actress who is always in the news,
Jodie Comer, and she sticks up for the Blues.

Advice on Writing a Poem about Liverpool

Avoid wet nellies like the plague,
and scouse should be off the menu.
Football if you must, but tread carefully,
for it can be a minefield. Put your foot
on the wrong colour and *Boom!*
You have written off half the population.

Doddy? Fine if you can come up with
an original thought, but leave the jokes
to him, and steer clear of naming
other comedians and entertainers,
lest you leave out somebody's favourite.

Wax lyrical about the music scene
at your peril. The Cavern? Yawn.
The Beatles? Admittedly at its core,
but can you say something that hasn't
been said a thousand times before?

The accent? Hard to describe without
sounding either tone deaf or superior.
Remember, it is music to native ears,
and on no account quote examples
when reading the poem aloud.

Although doubtful if thieves, thugs,
and drug dealers will read the poem,
one of them may have an aunty who does.
So, give them a wide berth just in case.
Talking of which, hard cases
with hearts of gold no longer exist,
the gold, nicked or sold ages ago.

The Liver Birds and the River Mersey?
The slave trade, Irish immigration and the Blitz?
If you can google it, leave it out.
Instead, write a poem about being alive
and feeling good about yourself.
Call it 'Liverpool'.

Advice on Writing a Poem for a Royal Occasion

First and foremost, decide who you are writing for.
Members of the Royal household, or its loyal
subjects, many of whom will not have English
as their first language? Perhaps you wish to impress
fellow poets, or literary critics, most of whom
are lining up to proclaim your homage execrable?

If you are writing for the monarch, bear in mind
that reigning supreme is time-consuming,
so keep it short. Not haiku-short, however,
and resist the lure of the limerick, thus avoiding
the temptation of inserting a vulgar pun in the last line.
Why not play it safe and opt for a Shakespearean sonnet?
With easy rhymes and a nod to one's noble forebears
you will be home and dry.

If you are writing for the general public,
do so at the kitchen table with a nice cup of tea
and Elgar playing in the background.
Appeal to the child in us all and touch the heartstrings.
God may be referred to, but only obliquely,
for fear of giving offence where none was intended.
Bring in corgis, but only if you must.

If you are writing to please fellow poets and critics,
ignore all the above and don't give up the day job.
Good luck!

Advice on Writing a Poem about the Pandemic

To revive the vibe and enhance the angst,
close the curtains, stop the clocks, and isolate
wearing a flimsy face mask of the period

Avoid statistics. Unless your readers
speak fluent mathematics, numbers may implode
within the brain, initiating flight mode

Don't blame raw meat or Satan,
politicians or paedophiles
In this case the culprit is a virus

Don't blame the virus. Regard
its psychotic behaviour as a challenge
to human ingenuity and the great unvaxxed

On a personal level, I feel deeply sorry
for your loss. But one day hopefully,
it will be found and handed in

In years to come when a child asks,
'What did you do during the Great Pandemic?'
You can say, 'Shit myself like everybody else.'

Time now to send the poem packing
and hope it doesn't come back to haunt you.
Finished? Then go and wash your hands.

Advice on Writing a Poem

I'd rather you didn't.
Unless you are doing it for granny's
birthday which is bound to please,
or for a bet, in which case you can fake it.
Or as part of an academic assignment
in which case you can follow up
with a decent bog-standard essay.

I'd rather you didn't.
There are so many out there
and although yours will be unique and special
because it echoes your voice and yours alone,
and reflects your narrative and yours alone,
I fear we may have read it many times,
many, many times.

Of course, some people think they know better.
Cooper Clarke, Hegley, Liz Berry, Agard,
Antrobus, Caroline Bird, Helen Mort,
Hollie McNish, the McMillans, Zephaniah,
Kae Tempest and Amanda Gorman
all came running for advice, and I told them,
I'd rather you didn't. But would they listen?

Fingers Crossed

Sorry not to have written anything for your anthology
But you know what it's like at this time of the year.
School exams and then straight into the holidays.
(A fortnight in Cornwall. Rain, rain, rain!)

Of course, I've seen the reports on television.
Did you know I was there some years ago?
A literary festival, of which I have fond memories.
(Though, in retrospect, a PR job for the regime.)

As you rightly point out, what is going on is tragic
And more needs to be done to help those suffering.
Especially the children. It is reassuring to know
That your book may help raise awareness.

As well as lots of money. Fingers crossed!
If you are planning a similar collection next year
(If not for this disaster, then for the next)
Please don't hesitate to get in touch.

Homophones in the Laundrette

Two of a kind, we have so much in common
I thought, as I cycled past him on the Common

Our bags were stuffed with soiled belongings
Was he lonely too? Filled with untold longings?

I could write a tune, a poem or a play for him,
Knowing that soon I would make a play for him

Although we had met only moments ago
Once inside, I decided to give it a go

Cried: 'Let's put our clothes into the same wash!'
The look of horror told me that it wouldn't wash

'Let's save time and money. Share our washing powder.'
But he turned his back and snapped, 'Take a powder.'

He needed his own machine. To run his own cycle
So rebuffed and unheeded, I rode home on my cycle.

Harbouring a Grudge

At anchor between the dinghies
and little yachts that sun themselves
and sway to the rhythm of the waves.

The Grudge is motionless.
Lying in the shadow of the sea wall, impatient
for its cargo of resentment to be unloaded.

Late in the afternoon, fishing boats return
after a busy day frisking the ocean
a screech of seagulls welcoming them home.

No seagulls for the Grudge
only an unkindness of ravens
that caw, kraa and strut upon the deck.

Angry, confused and impatient
he heads for the Harbour Master's office.
'Where did it come from? How long will it be here?'

Without knocking he barges in.
She looks up from the desk. 'Come to say sorry?'
Realising that he had, he takes her hand.

Through the window beyond the bay
a smudge on the distant horizon.
The Grudge evaporating into darkness.

The Good Ship Attenborough

(Launched by Sir David in Birkenhead, July 2018)

There's excitement in Antarctica
a saviour is on the way
Half-man, half-ship, in coat of red
who vows to save the day

A man of steel, with heart of gold
and brain the size of Hyde Park
Rides the flood like Noah
on a recommissioned Ark

With damage to the environment
and global warming on his mind
The mission, not yet impossible,
to save the planet and mankind

Not for money, power or glory,
plain truth the only prize
There's expectation in the deep
and excitement in the skies

Beneath the melting ice
dolphins, seals and whales
Swim round and round in circles
clapping fins and waggling tails

Penguins prance and pirouette
and all the birds of the air
Keep their feathers crossed
as they offer up a prayer

For the good ship *Attenborough*
and her dedicated crew
Seeking evidence that will terrify
for only then might we renew

Our promise to leave the Earth
perhaps a better place
For the sake of our children's children
and the future of our race

The sea is rising, the message is clear
have we time to rewind the clock?
Shhh . . . Listen, what do we hear?
Antarc tic . . . toc . . . *tic* . . . *toc* . . . *tic* . . . *toc* . . . *tic* . . . *tic* . . . *tic* . . .

Voice Over

Bet on a horse, bet on the game
Lose all your money? Terrible shame
You're the mug, I'm not to blame
I'm only the voice. The voice over.

Hit the jackpot twice this week?
Double your ackers, on a winning streak . . .
Oh no, bad luck! You're up shit creek
But don't point at me, I'm only the voice, the voice over.

As much excitement as you'll get
Re-mortgage the house for one last bet . . .
Oh no, how sad! In serious debt
But don't blame me, I'm only the voice, the voice over.

I'm just part of an ad campaign
If the money's right I'll do it again
(Though drawing the line at guns and cocaine)
I'm not the brain, I'm only the voice, the voice over.

Nobody gets to see my face
No clues to religion, class or race
Anonymous, so I'm not to blame.
Where's the shame? I'm only the voice, the voice over.

You've lost your home, you've lost your wife
Nothing left? You can bet on your life . . .
Oh no, you've lost it! Now Bet in Peace
But I'm not to blame, I'm only the voice
The voice over . . . the voice over . . . the voice over . . .

And remember, when the fun stops . . .
We don't.

A Fresh Coat of Paint

'I care about the environment

That poem about the paranoid father
building a fall-out shelter during the Cuban Crisis.
A deranged Noah adrift in a nuclear nightmare
was a chilling image in the sixties. But now?

and try to do what is right.

President Nixon, desperate to hang on to power,
brought the curtain up on shenanigans
outside the White House. A grotesque pantomime
that seemed funny at the time. But now?

So, I cycle to work every morning

Boy meets girl in laundrette. Add a gender spin.
Swap a pan of scouse for a plate of haggis.
Not a day to be found in possession of conkers
or committing adultery, ask the old Manxman.

and recycle home every night.'

The poet as re-cyclist.
The joys of self-plagiarism. Fresh coat of paint, etc.

Where the Sun Don't Shine

Lewis Gibbons repeatedly knifed a teenager,
leaving him to die alone in a pool of blood.
As he was sent down for a minimum of 21 years,
Gibbons smirked and showed his middle finger
to stunned onlookers, including the victim's family.

Some months later in Walton Prison
two inmates, one of them an uncle of the deceased,
gained access to his cell. After overpowering
him they hacked off his middle finger
and rammed the offending digit up his arse.

Following the operation, the surgeon explained
that the finger had been successfully removed
and once the tendons had been realigned
it could be re-grafted and put back into place.
Gibbons however, told him where to stick it.

Broads Don't Scare Easy

(featuring Doting Donald, Ruthless Ruth and Reckless Eric)

He worked in real estate and was doing rather well
She worked around the clock in a downtown sex motel
It was love at first transaction, and he became
besotted with this fallen angel, and soon his aim
was to rescue her. She played the victim to the hilt,
abused by men, wracked with shame and guilt.
Who would save this wretched sinner, lost and weak?
He assumed the missionary position, so to speak.

Donald Steiner became increasingly bewitched
by his young wife Ruth. She could twist herself
round his little finger, and so he was more than happy
to sign a life insurance policy for fifty thousand dollars
(including a double-indemnity clause in the event
of violent death). All for love. But love is blind they say,
and accidents do happen, so perhaps doting Donald
might be excused for failing to notice a sinister pattern
emerging in the catalogue of mishaps that followed:

Like almost suffocating in bed when Ruth had gone
for a walk, forgetting to light the gas fire after turning
on the taps. Bumping into her on deck while cleaning
his boat and falling overboard. Like being nearly crushed
under the Buick while changing the wheel, the jack
inexplicably sliding away after she had walked past.
Collapsing after being given unlabelled cough medicine.
Like being overcome by carbon monoxide fumes
when the garage door became locked from the outside.

While Donald doted, Ruth plotted. She had a plan
and what it needed was a man. Enter Eric Carr,
gambler, would-be actor, and small-time hustler
with an eye for the ladies and a nose for the coke.
Five years younger, he bought into her Technicolor
dream of a life together in the hills near Hollywood.
The plan devised was foolproof: A bungled burglary.
Middle of the night, and the husband clubbed to death.

2 a.m. Sunday May 20th 1927, a house on Long Island.
While drunken Donald snored, Ruth slipped out of bed,
crept downstairs and let in her accomplice, stoned
and terrified at the thought of the gruesome task ahead.
Ruth, however, excited at the prospect of widowhood,
bundled him upstairs, handed him an electric cord
and whispered, 'Strangle him.' When Donald resisted
and Eric looked on in horror, she grabbed a heavy
brass crucifix with both hands and shattered his skull.

After knocking over a few chairs, opening some drawers,
tousling Ruth's hair, smacking her on the arms and cheek
before tying her up, Eric fled the scene. The perfect crime.
And it would have been, had the police not interfered.
No signs of a break-in, is that what concerned them?
Was it the looseness of the ropes that bound her?
Or the lack of bruising and injuries? The items reported
stolen being found hidden in the attic? And Eric, holed up
in a motel downtown, broken and desperate to confess.

In court, the once fallen angel, now a church-going,
home-loving, and neglected wife, shed martyr's tears
and pointed the finger at Eric, the cruel, manipulative
alcoholic who had devised and carried out the deed.
After hearing the evidence, the jury chatted, smoked,
and gave its verdict. Eric would meet Old Sparky first,
but for St Ruth the Innocent, not Sing Sing but Calvary,
the black execution hood, her crown of thorns:
'Father forgive them, for they know not what they do.'

FX: A Ghost Story

Toby Farnham, crouched over the wheel of his TR2,
was not enjoying the ride. Visibility was down
to a few metres as the fog arched its back
against the windscreen like a fat grey weasel.
Outside, a distant church clock chimed the hour,
but the only sound he could hear was the steady
hum of his finely tuned engine and the incessant
swish of the windscreen wipers.

At this rate he'd never make the studio in time
to finish the programme due for transmission the
following night. In an attempt to dispel his gloom,
Toby switched on the car radio and sang along
to his favourite Beatles track. Suddenly,
and without warning, the car spluttered to a halt.
He cursed softly to himself. 'Running out of petrol
in filthy weather and in the middle of nowhere.'

He switched off the ignition, the windscreen wipers
and the radio. Should I ring the studio and tell them
to start editing *FX: A Ghost Story* without me?
No, I'll get there, and work through the night
if I have to. Rather than sit imprisoned in his car
he decided to brave the elements in the hope
of finding a garage, a farmhouse. Anything.
He took a deep breath and got out.

The fog leaped upon him, its paws
on his shoulders, clinging to him, pushing
its cold tongue into his nose and ears.
He stumbled on blindly. The only sounds
he could hear were his own muffled footsteps
and the occasional hoot of a distant owl.
He was just on the point of resigning himself
to the end of a promising career in radio

when straight ahead he could dimly make out
the blurred outline of a building. Too big
for a farmhouse. Manor house more like,
even some sort of church. No lights on
anywhere. He groped along the outside
looking for an entrance. He found it.
A heavy wooden door slightly ajar. Putting
his left shoulder to it, he pushed and pushed.

It creaked slowly open. He was in just in time
as the door clanged shut behind him.
Strangely there was no handle on the inside.
It was pitch black and wherever he was,
he was locked in. He cursed softly to himself.
Unable to see anything in the eerie blackness
he shuffled forward like a blindfolded three-year-old
wearing his father's shoes. His left elbow

brushed against something cold and hard.
And then he heard it: The laughter, cruel,
bloodcurdling. He turned, and as he did
collided into what seemed like a coffin.
A werewolf howled. Panicking, he ran.
Footsteps echoed after him. Thunder rumbled
all around. The wind roared. He crashed
into a wall. There could be no escape!

In his mind's eye, he saw the Thing coming
towards him. Half-man. Half-beast, half-pissed.
Panic-stricken, he dug his fingernails into the wall.
A headless rider on a phantom horse galloped
into view, followed by a band of Indians
hotly pursued by the 14th Cavalry. The 7.55
from St Pancras, dead on time, rattled through.
Hands over his ears, he screamed: 'Stop! Stop! Stop!'

And that was how they found him next morning. Dead,
in the sound effects department of Broadcasting House.

Let me take you for a walk.
Yes, you.
Give me your hand.
We will be joined later
by another former
school teacher,
then a family of five
who lived above
the nail bar
on the corner
by the level-crossing.
Yes, tragic,
but there you are.
A geriatric nurse,
and then by pure
coincidence, a detour
to a care home
where we can expect
some delay.
Then an actor,
quite famous
apparently.
Then a bus driver
and a bishop.
Yes, a bishop.
Single file, everybody,
cemetery coming up
on the left-hand side,
so, please keep
the noise down
as we file past.
Just up ahead
you will see the end
of the queue
which you must join.
Yes, as you say,
it does seem
to stretch into infinity.
But this is where
I must leave you.
Goodbye.

Let me take you for a walk.
Yes, you.
Give me your hand.
We will be joined shortly
by a hairdresser
and then by
a publican whose wife
is in the queue
not far ahead.
Single file, everybody,
and stop when you reach
the level-crossing.
Ok. All clear
and over we go.
See the nail bar
on the corner?
Refugee family
living above.
Sad story.
At the junction
we slow down
for an ex-RAF
fighter pilot
to climb aboard.
What tales
he could tell, eh?
How long have I
been doing this?
Since the first death
as a matter of fact.
But it's a long story
and you're about
to join another queue.
No, they're not
always as long
as this, you've
joined us at a
particularly busy time.
And this is where
I must leave you.
Goodbye.

Let me take you for a walk.
Yes, you.
Give me your hand.
How long in the job?
Since death began
as a matter of fact.
I was the first human
to take a life.
The original murderer.
I take no credit for it,
and the whys
and wherefores
I don't remember,
but it was quick.
You can look it up
if you're interested.
Once the blood gates
were opened
all was chaos
so, I was called in
to provide order,
along with others
who had killed
and not repented.
That was the deal,
take a life
and be punished
by spending eternity
in *postmortal*.
In my case, as a guide,
others in security,
border control,
that sort of thing.
Safety in Numbers
you might say.
And this is where
I must leave you.
Just up ahead
is the queue
that you must join.
Goodbye.

Let me take you for a walk.
Yes, you
and you
and you
and you
and you
and you
and you
and you
and you
and you
and you
and you
and you
and you
and you
and you
and you
and you
and you
and you
and you
and you
and you
and you
and you
and you
and you
and you
and you
and you
and you
and you
and you
and you
and you
and you
and you
and you
and you
and you
and you
and you.
Yes, you.

Another Year, Another Bicycle

What was it like for you
When twenty-twenty
left its bicycle outside on the step?

Did you rush out and bring it in?
Or were you laid low? On the front line
perhaps, helping stem the flow?

And what will you remember of the year,
as if I didn't know? The parties, the weddings,
the trips abroad? Let me hazard a guess . . . no?

The sudden fear of losing family members
long since dead. In mourning for loved ones
very much alive and therefore vulnerable

The contagion of fear. Did you remember
to wash your hands after saying your prayers?
Lost in a thickening haze of bewilderment

Lockdowns and letdowns, lecterns and tiers
The relentless profusion of daphs and grata
An endless confusion of chigures and farts

Round after brutal round, but still on its feet,
as whistling a tune yet to be written,
Tiny Tim comes wobbling down the street.

Acknowledgements

I wish to thank my editor, Mary Mount; my agent, Charles Walker at United Agents; my Italian translator, Franco Nasi; my long-serving manager and fellow poet, Adrian Mealing; and all the readers and listeners who have supported me over the years.

Self-acknowledgements

The author would also like to thank his younger self for permission to revive and revise poems that have been previously published:

'Just Another Autumn Day', 'Incident at a Presidential Garden Party' (*Holiday on Death Row*, 1979). 'Noah's Ark' (*Waving at Trains*, 1982). 'Today is Not a Day for Adultery', 'Q' (*Melting into the Foreground*, 1986). 'On the Point of Extinction', 'On Having a First Book of Poetry Published' (*Everyday Eclipses*, 2002). 'Scouse-power' (*Good Enough to Eat*, 2002). 'Love in the Laundrette' (*That Awkward Age*, 2009).